RESPECT HIM

By
CRYSTAL JONES

Copyright © 2020 Respect Him by Crystal Jones

All rights reserved.

This work may not be used in any form, or reproduced by any means, in whole or in part, without written permission from the publisher or author.

All scripture references are from King James Version unless otherwise stated.

Edited, formatted, and published by

Destiny House Publishing, LLC.

P.O. Box 19774

Detroit, MI 48219

404.993.0830

www.destinyhousepublishing.com

email: inquiry@destinyhousepublishing.com

Cover Design by Kingdom Graphics Designs

All rights reserved.

ISBN-13: 978-1-936867-58-5

DEDICATION

I dedicate this book to my 3 fabulous, loving, and fearless daughters,
Kyria, Charity, and LaTina.
You mean more to me than I can articulate. I am grateful to God for such precious gifts. I relish in your love, smiles, and laughter; as you are my joy and inspiration. I see a little bit of myself in each of you. My prayer is that you would be amazing daughters of God, affording you to become the best wives you could possibly be. I love you, bunches.

I also dedicate this book to my lovely daughter-in-law, Keila, the wife of an amazing husband and my precious princess of a goddaughter, Sara Ann Miller.

I pray that you will all be 'Dream Wives' to your husbands (Charity, Keila, and Sara) and future husbands (Kyria, and LaTina) and offer them the respect and honor that God requests of you.

Great things are in your future. When you make your husband the king of your castle, you position yourself as queen. So adjust his crown and watch your relationship soar.

CONTENTS

ACKNOWLEDGMENTS i

INTRODUCTION 3

1 RESPECT YOURSELF 7

2 FROM BOYS TO MEN 21

3 DOES HE DESERVE IT? 33

4 WHAT ABOUT ME? 43

5 WHAT IF HE'S WRONG? 53

6 THINK LIKE A WOMAN 63

7 OUT OF CONTROL 73

8 BODY MINISTRY 81

9 HIS DREAM WIFE 87

10 THE BEST PART 98

ABOUT THE AUTHOR 101

ACKNOWLEDGMENTS

I give honor to the Eternal Head of my life and Savior of my Soul, my Lord, and Lover, Jesus Christ. Thank you for saving me and healing and blessing my union. The journey has been incredible because of You. I feel so honored that you trust me to be the helpmeet of such an amazing man. Thank you for calling us to this ministry. It is my pleasure to lead others as you lead me. It is my joy to love, respect and honor you forever.

I also honor my Alpha Male, the greatest man on the planet, Oscar L. Jones, for being my lover, encourager, and partner in ministry. You are my muse. I am hopelessly in love with you. It is a pleasure to submit to your authority. I trust you completely. Thank you for making it so easy.

INTRODUCTION

"The truest form of love is how you behave toward someone, not how you feel about them."
— **Steve Hall**

Disrespect usually shows itself in put-downs, yelling, name-calling, usurping authority, contradicting, overriding a decision, ridicule, sarcasm, etc. As a result, the recipient is usually embarrassed.

To embarrass: to cause confusion and shame; to make uncomfortably self-conscious; disconcert; abash: to cause to experience a state of self-conscious distress.

No one likes to be embarrassed. It makes us all self-conscious. As bad as it is for women, it's much worse for men. Experiencing public humiliation for men is ranked a close second place to death, in the worse things that could happen to them. To embarrass him is to diminish him and make him look weak. And the worse person to receive that disgrace from is his one flesh partner.

Most times, women don't understand how injurious shame is for their men. I think if we understood it, we would be less likely to commit such a grievous treason. It is not our intention to render such a shattering blow to our husband's ego. Sometimes we are completely oblivious to the sword we've just wielded. And we find it difficult to understand why our husbands are aloof or guarded. But it is usually because his wife has harmed him emotionally.

In all honesty, the wife is usually trying to get her husband to understand a point or see a different perspective. However, if she doesn't speak the language of respect, she will not be able

INTRODUCTION

to communicate with her husband properly. It requires that she stops to think about her words and pray about the best way to do that.

Proverbs admonish us to be slow to speak and quick to hear. It also says that a word spoken in due season how good it is. We have to take time to think about what we will say and *how* we will say it.

Love equals respect to a man. If a man doesn't feel respected, he most certainly does not feel loved.

Men are not like women. The two are different in the way they see things and process them. That is not a negative. That's just what it is. If we seek to understand our spouses, our differences can make us better. We can bring strength to the places our husbands are weak and vice versa.

Ultimately love is shown in action. It's not about the love we feel towards our husbands but the love we express.

Loving him requires that we keep our husbands' dignity intact. Therefore it is incumbent upon us to go to great lengths to avoid shaming him. If not, we could cause irreparable damage to our unions.

I desire to help you better understand your husband and other men in your life. I pray that you learn principles and be equipped with tools to help you grow in your relationship. And prayerfully, this journey will lead you to become an incredible blessing to your husband.

It has been said that a man's best friend is his dog. But I pray that your husband's best friend is his godly wife gifted to him from God. Be the woman he can safely trust. Support him and help him to shine.

May you never shame your husband or any other man in your life. And may your husband declare that you are the best thing that ever happened to him.

1
RESPECT YOURSELF

The need to humiliate and shame another human being is not a reflection of them, but a reflection of you.
- Unknown

'Respect Yourself' is the name of a classic soul song by American rhythm & blues/gospel group, The Staple Singers. It was released in late 1971. The message in the lyrics is as relevant to our culture today, as it was back then. We can't respect others until we respect ourselves.

Respect is fundamental to community. And yet, it seems to be not esteemed or practiced in our culture. We don't respect God. We have little respect for authority, and consequently, we don't respect each other. Race, religion, gender, political parties, and other issues divide us. We are not civil enough to agree to disagree.

Sadly, in today's climate, disagreement yields disrespect. We are not mature enough to respect someone else's different point of view. This is not just true of the world, but unfortunately, it is also true of the church.

God requires respect of us all, not to be directed to Himself only, but he requires that we would extend it to each other as our moral currency. Respect has to begin with individuals to positively affect our culture.

When we get on our platforms, we like to speak of an ambiguous "they" who seem to be responsible for every ill in our society. It is unproductive to talk about what "they" should be doing or how "they" should conduct themselves when we are offenders. Our society is quite judgmental. We point our fingers and say what others ought to be doing; while we make the same infractions. We can't change our world until we change ourselves. We must take a serious look in the mirror.

Every person on the earth is due respect. Though some would tout that respect has to be earned. From a biblical perspective, that is not true. God asks us to give respect to even those who do not act respectfully.

If we, as the church, are ever going to impact the world, we must live what we say we believe. That means instead of policing what everyone else is doing, we must be the first partaker of the fruit. We must offer respect to others. It's how we treat those that we encounter that matters.

The only way to see change emerge, we all must be willing to take action in our own lives about the way we speak and behave toward others. As someone once said, I must be the change I want to see in the world, in my community and my marriage.

A neck-bobbing, eye-rolling, finger-pointing, sarcastic, critical woman is not what a husband hopes to find in his wife. Neither is it the type of woman a wife hopes to see in herself. To a husband, it can feel like the old 'bait-and-switch' tactic. It's a type of fraud where you are promised one thing but then offered something inferior. It would do us well to ask ourselves, "Am I the type of wife that my husband was expecting on my wedding day?"

As I have ministered around the country, I've heard wives say, "He takes me there, or he makes me act out of character." Of course, this is *not* true. This is simply a justification to excuse ungodly behavior. As God's daughters, we have to take responsibility for our actions. We can't assign blame to our husbands when it is we that behave unseemly.

The God who tells us to love those who are unlovable, also tells us to exercise *self-control*. We don't get to render evil for evil if our husband is demonstrating less than honorable behavior. On the contrary, we are to overcome evil with good to inherit the blessing (I Peter 3:9).

Wisdom nudges us to give a soft or gentle answer in response to anger. But if our words are grievous, they will certainly provoke anger in our mates (Proverbs 15:1).

So blaming our husbands doesn't excuse us. We must first own our actions if we want to see change in our marriages. If I am disrespectful, the fault lies with me. No one can <u>force</u> me to be disrespectful. It is the reaction I default to. When put in a situation, we either default to the spirit or the flesh. It will depend on which one is more alive. We have to know carnal responses produce no good fruit.

The recipient of insult-laced words is usually left feeling stung and belittled. Husbands tend to withdraw into an invisible shell when attacked. So when a wife "snaps" on her husband or gets him told, he will venture out a little less often. Like a turtle, he will withdraw into his shell when he feels unsafe. He will be agreeable only in words. He can no longer confide in his wife because it is not safe to do so.

The ill-mannered wife teaches her husband to distrust her when she comes to him with a verbal assault. She is unlike the Proverbs 31 wife, whose husband safely trusts in her (Proverbs 31:11).

She doesn't understand that devaluing her husband, is an affront to herself. I've witnessed women publicly disrespecting their husbands. And while her pummeling is directed at him, to all others, she is the one who looks foolish. She appears disheveled and rude.

One such couple was at the airport. The husband had misplaced his boarding pass, and his outraged wife was loud and demeaning. After telling him how incompetent he was, she then lined up to board the plane, leaving her husband to figure it out for himself.

He seemed a timid man, flustered and embarrassed. Many of the other passengers came to his assistance and told him to go to the counter. The poor guy went to the counter, and the kind flight attendants issued him another boarding pass. In no time at all, he was able to board the plane with the rest of us.

It is unfortunate that the airline employees and passengers were kinder to this woman's husband than the one who promised to love and honor him. This wife needed some real training. She was doing great harm to her marriage. Perhaps she was embarrassed that her husband had been a little absent-minded. And maybe he had been absent-minded many times before. This was still no excuse for her blatant disrespect.

We all have some areas that we need to grow in. It's not just husbands that need to grow. Wives have issues, too. All have sinned and fell short of God's glory. This woman should have offered her husband a little more grace and tried to find out what they could do together to fix the problem, instead of getting in line without him. I am sure if asked, she would say that humans should respect one another. Unfortunately, that is not how she was choosing to conduct herself. What we say and what we do must align. When those two are congruent, then we operate in integrity.

I often wonder if brash wives could handle the harsh words and hurtful actions that they dish out to their husbands. If the shoe were on the other foot, it would be interesting to see how the wife would respond. We should talk to our husbands like we want them to speak to us.

One can surmise by her actions that the woman at the airport was quite insecure. She was trying to gain control over the situation with her husband. When a woman is insecure, she does not feel safe and will most often do whatever it takes to move herself to a safer space. No matter how harmful her actions may be.

Unfortunately, that wife thought of herself first above her husband. She was trying to cover herself in an uncomfortable position. However, proper respect deems that she consider him first. He was in a vulnerable position. Instead of making him feel worse, her role as his wife was to support him and help him feel better.

When men are at their *least*, that's when they need the 'most' respect from their wives. That's worth repeating. *Men need affirmation and encouragement from their wives when they mess up and are most vulnerable.* Ironically, the opposite is what happens too often.

Think about how your life would change if you covered your husband in his weakness. If you show mercy and kindness to your husband when he messes up, he will draw closer to you. He will feel covered by his wife and hold his head up a little higher. Love really does cover.

A woman who respects herself will not find it as challenging to show honor to her husband. Respecting yourself means understanding your value. It is carrying yourself with dignity and exercising self-control. You don't stoop low to be disparaging to others when you love yourself. The Golden Rule tells us to treat others as we want to be treated (Matthew 7:12). It's our default. And it's how God expects us to respond to others.

I encountered another woman in a grocery store, yelling at her husband for all the world to hear. His face was beet red. I didn't know what he had done that she thought reason enough to publicly humiliate her husband. If she had taken a moment to look up, she would have seen the nasty looks she was getting from the customers pushing their carts around hers. He was the one embarrassed, but she was the one getting the snide looks.

She missed an opportunity to draw her husband closer. When we understand that we pull our husbands closer to us with honor and respect, we will choose what is supernatural above that which is natural.

Maybe you have never publicly humiliated your husband. If that's so, good for you. But if you have ever been guilty of doing so privately or even in your mind, that is still undesirable behavior. We have to live what we say we believe. It starts with showing respect to God and to ourselves.

Often we project on others how we feel about ourselves. We all have a code of conduct that we live by. It is how we know how to treat ourselves and others. We operate from those core values. If we are patient, gentle, long-suffering, and loving toward ourselves, then we will extend the same courtesy to others. The way we treat others is a real reflection of how we feel about ourselves. When we are rude and disrespectful toward others, it is a symptom of the secret insecurity that lies within us. And it will betray us every time. Insecurity makes a person grasp for control. A wife who doesn't feel safe, protected, or secure will grab control for herself at the expense of most anyone else involved.

You respect yourself by living your core values. As a child of the King, you represent not just yourself, but the King of kings. The daughter of the King does not act unseemly. She is always mindful of the One she represents.

Now then we are ambassadors for Christ, as though God did beseech you by us: we pray you in Christ's stead, be ye reconciled to God. II Corinthians 5:20 KJV

Respect requires actually putting the Word into practice in our lives and relationships. It's not enough to say you respect your husband. He must see it and feel it.

RESPECT YOURSELF

There are many Christians who are so in name only. You don't see the attributes of Christianity in their behavior or responses. They exercise no restraint or control over their flesh. They react, and it's usually not good.

We don't get to act up and think God is okay with it. His bar is set high, and He doesn't lower his standards because we are in a mood or angry.

Respecting one's self requires that we receive God's gifts for ourselves and then proceed to give them to others. Those gifts are His lavish unconditional love, limitless forgiveness and mercy, his extravagant grace, mind-blowing peace and strengthening joy. All of these amazing gifts are for all of us. We must first partake of them and then we can pour them out on others. If we never receive them for ourselves, we can't give what we don't have. Only a graceful person can give grace. Is your grace-full? A peaceful person can bring peace to a challenge. Is your peace on full? Or are you on empty?

RESPECT HIM

Everything hinges on us developing our relationship with God. God can replenish us if we ask him. If you need more forgiveness, draw it down for yourself. Whatever is lacking, God is willing and available to supply.

If you are a wife who has not received God's gifts for yourself, ask Him for help. Allow the Lord to heal you and then surrender every insecurity to Him. Take time to learn and live respect for yourself. As you learn to lean on the Lord and trust Him in all things, you will be a valuable asset to your husband.

2
FROM BOYS TO MEN

When I was a child, I spake as a child, I understood as a child, I thought as a child: but when I became a man, I put away childish things.
I Corinthians 13:11 KJV

Over the years, I've encountered many wives who describe their husbands as children. Most often, it is spoken in jest and in the company of other women. However, even if he is not present, it still reeks of contempt. Something within you should set off an alarm, "I shouldn't say this."

Boys don't get married. Men do. And it's quite dishonorable to the head of your household to refer to him as such. Not only do you diminish him in the eyes of the person you are speaking to, but you affect your own image of him. Words are spirit.

Your husband is not your child. It is illogical to treat your husband like a child, then expect him to act like a man. If a wife handles her husband with reverence, he will often respond in kind. If she regards him as a child, she should expect him to behave like one. You sow the seed you want to reap. Sow love and honor you will reap a king. Sow disregard and contempt, and you will reap an angry tyrant or a bitter, emasculated passive-aggressive man.

Men resent being treated like children. Your husband is a fully mature adult perfectly capable of authentic manhood. The woman who thinks her husband is childish has a husband with a childish wife.

It is not a woman's responsibility to teach her husband how to be a man, just as a husband cannot teach his wife about femininity. A man learns authentic manhood best from his relationship with God and through other men.

It is an unwise woman who thinks that her husband can be mothered into being a good husband. He cannot. And he will not. He does not want another mother, especially as a wife.

If a husband is being beaten down by his wife's harsh and condescending words, he will sometimes become passive-aggressive. It's his way of responding to an overbearing/controlling wife. He resists her attacks and attempts at making him over by shutting down.

This controlling type of wife shifts into the role of a maternal figure in the marriage, because she rejects her husband as he is and his way of doing things. So she tries to reform him. It's an effort for her to regain control. She feels uncomfortable, at risk, or untrusting. So she reprimands, corrects, criticizes, and scolds him like a 3-year-old.

With each irreverent deed, she is chipping away a little piece of his ego. A man's ego is attached to his image and how he sees himself, which makes it hard to connect to her. So she unwittingly cuts his connection to her. When she is done, she will have removed the intimacy from their marriage. And he will grow cold and distant towards her.

The overbearing wife emasculates her husband in her struggle for power. She may say she wants him to lead, but she only wants him to lead *the way she wants him to lead*. If his suggestions are contrary to what she thinks they should do, she will reject his leadership. She is adverse to surrendering control. It's too frightening. It makes her feel too defenseless.

And so they enter this vicious cycle. She resists, and he resents. It's a battle for the reins. Both want to lead the marriage, but there can only be one leader. Two visions in marriage result in a divided vision or division. They will find themselves going in two different directions.

The husband with a controlling wife will settle back into passive behavior. He will refuse to lead or he leads from an inert posture.

Passive aggressiveness is non-verbal aggression that manifests in negative, immature behavior. The husband is silently angry. He appears to be in agreement, but he is not. He goes along to get along. As one husband put it, he goes along for the sake of peace. But it's a false peace.

Men don't like to engage in confrontation with their women. So when a man lets his wife have her way, it's a sign that he has given up. He doesn't want to expend the energy to lead, so he withdraws emotionally.

This destructive behavior cycle continues if the wife insists on mothering her husband. She treats him like a child, so he resists like an impudent child. Her actions yield her the opposite desired behavior. She won't ever get what she really wants because she is going about it in the wrong way.

It's not a wife's job to tell her husband what to do. It is her primary job to pray for him. And encourage him to seek God for direction. She is to be a team player and not buck against his leadership.

It has been said that men are not emotional. Men don't display their emotions like women, but men are indeed emotional beings. Men are emotional because they are created in the likeness and image of God. And God is emotional. We see God demonstrating emotions of anger, compassion, joy, love, etc.

Men can be very sensitive. An overbearing wife can easily injure their feelings. It is difficult for a man to stand up against the venom of a wife with a bitter tongue. He is usually no match for her. And her beaten-down husband will slip into silence.

A husband may be dying inside, but never share those feelings with his wife. He is taught to stuff his emotions, hide, and be tough on the exterior. And so that's what many men do. They take a licking and keep on ticking…like a time bomb. It's just a matter of time before an explosion occurs.

God created the wife to be an anointed helper to her husband, not a hurtful helper. She must help him in the way God intended, not how she decides. Believe in him, inspire him and cheer him on. Her words and behavior should lift him up and not tear him down. She should offer him the honor that God says he is due.

When your husband was a boy, the woman in the helper position was his mother. But when a boy becomes a man, his helper is his wife. And he no longer needs his mother in the same way. That is why he is told to "leave his mother and father and cleave to his wife." (Genesis 2:24 KJV). His wife is to be the one he holds on to.

It's important to understand that a husband **leaves** his mother and cleaves to a wife. If the wife acts as his mother, she pushes him away from her. If she acts as his wife, he draws closer to her.

God never intended that wives would *mother* their husbands. This is not in divine order. The marriage relationship is comprised of a husband and a wife, not a husband and a mother. If a wife takes on the motherly role, her husband will rebel against her. Her disrespectful behavior will not yield her the love and attention that she needs.

A husband's actions are not a total measurement of his manhood. He will grow into his manhood, just like we as women grow into our womanhood. But there has to be grace in the marriage to grow. We don't start out in the marriage where we will end up. Thank God for that! We will mature and gain understanding along the way. The person we've chosen to journey through this life will help us, and we will help them.

A prudent wife is from the Lord (Proverbs 19:14). The prudent wife gets this.

Proverbs 12:4 says A virtuous woman is a crown to her husband: but she that maketh ashamed is as rottenness in his bones.

The prudent wife **doesn't** talk down to her husband:

"Start acting like a man…"

"If you were a real man, you would…"

"Don't be so stupid!"

"You are such a jerk!"

These are demeaning words spoken out of frustration. But they leave a nasty impact on the marriage. To operate like a prudent wife, you must be slow to speak, especially when feeling a barrage of emotions. You don't want to negatively and permanently impact your relationship over a temporary feeling.

When he messes up, the prudent wife offers her husband the same grace that God offers her. She doesn't wish him evil or harms him with the tongue that was meant to bless him. She openeth her mouth with wisdom; and in her tongue is the law of kindness. (Proverbs 31:26 KJV)

We must respond in the way God wants us to and not the way we _feel_. Maturity provokes us to operate with patience and gentleness.

A man's ego is a necessary part of who he is. I once heard a wife say that she had to stick a pin in her husband's head because his ego was too big. I gently corrected her. "That is the job of the Holy Spirit. Your job is to be his helper." We don't get to bruise our husband's ego because he's feeling himself. Men were created with ego. It is his drive. The ego is like the engine in a car. Once it gets going, you don't want to stop it. If you shut the engine down, you shut the entire car down.

Certainly a man's ego needs to be sanctified. Sanctification is the job of the Holy Spirit. So we can't take the place of God. The Holy Spirit knows how to sanctify that ego. Wives must learn to trust the Lord in this. God knows how to get your husband, where he wants him to be.

Cultivate the traits you want to see in your husband through faith. If you want a strong man, treat him like he is a strong man. If you want a provider, lean on him to provide. If you want a leader, follow him.

Women need men. All women may not need a husband, but we all need men. We need our sons, fathers, grandfathers, brothers, uncles, nephews, etc. If they are in our lives, we will have to learn how to handle them properly. It's not just husbands that need respect, but all men. If we can learn to respect all humankind, our lives will certainly be better for it.

I Peter 2:17 reads, **Honour all men**. Love the brotherhood. Fear God. Honour the king.

Marriage is God's idea, and so it must be done His way. The blessing will rest upon you if you learn to reverence God, honor your king, and give respect to all humans.

3
DOES HE DESERVE IT?

Kindness is loving people more than they deserve.
— Joseph Joubert

We live in an era of entitlement. It's the American way. Advertisements constantly tell us we deserve some expensive vehicle or product. We are told to treat ourselves to some decadent dessert. While we may not be the most overweight and unhealthy nation, our numbers are still relatively high. We are overextended in debt because we consistently buy items we can't afford. "I deserve it" is the mantra. We are pushed to consume and the motivating force is – our own self-worth. Our culture tells us that, "We deserve it!" And we buy into it. "I must deserve things I can't afford; it's the American way."

So when we get married, our expectations are high and unrealistic. We expect the relationships of the movie screens with all the romance bells and whistles.

There have been so many wives who have complained that their young marriages (some not even 5 years) don't resemble that of marriages that are 30+ years. But they haven't yet put in the blood, sweat, and tears of those senior marriages.

All marriages are not equal. Family background, experiences, culture, knowledge, spiritual maturity, and the season you're in, all play a part in where you are in your relationship.

When wives have an entitlement attitude, there is little grace for their husbands. Because the idea is 'I deserve more than what he is giving!'

Many wives can rattle off a full list of what their husbands should and should not be doing for them. But her list would be scarce detailing what she should be doing or giving in the marriage. It's unbalanced thinking.

We come to the marriage with unrealistic expectations. The thing that we all need to understand about marriage is that we don't start with an amazing relationship with our spouses. We have to grow into it.

God's Word teaches us how to get there. Ephesians 5:33 reads Nevertheless let every one of you in particular so love his wife even as himself; **and the wife see that she reverence her husband (my emphasis).** It's plain and simple. The husband must love his wife, and the wife must reverence her husband. This is what we should be practicing every day. We won't master it right away. But it is our starting point.

God offers us his unconditional love. The God who loves us with no strings attached died on our behalf. He didn't wait until we were better to love us, but He loved us in spite of ourselves. He is a God who loves us - simply because we are created in his image and likeness. Whether we accept Him or not, Our Kind King still loves us. His love is not based upon our right behavior.

Now don't misunderstand. His promises are conditional. We have to obey Him to receive what He has for us. But His love is free-flowing and always available. And so when the Lord asks the husband to love His wife, He asks him to love her like He does. She doesn't have to earn his love. It is not based upon her conduct. It is a wedding gift - unconditional love that God expects every husband to render to his wife.

And in that same way, the wife is asked to offer to her husband a wedding gift – unconditional honor. No strings. No behavior is demanded in exchange for it. Simply respect him. Think about that for a moment. Your husband does not have to *deserve* honor or respect. He is due it, just as you as his wife do not have to earn his love. You are due love. You were both asked to render these gifts at the wedding altar. What a beautiful gift exchange! He gives love, and she gives respect, both unconditionally.

This is the beauty of marriage when both spouses can offer these gifts without expecting anything in return.

God is the one who asks you to submit and to reverence your husband. So every wife who loves and respects her God will respect her husband.

1 Peter 2:18 reads, Servants, be subject to your masters with all fear; **not only to the good and gentle**, but also to the froward. (Emphasis mine.)

1 Peter 3:1 reads, Likewise, ye wives, be in subjection to your own husbands; that, if any obey not the word, they also may without the word be won by the conversation of the wives;

In 1 Peter 2:18, Peter starts out talking to servants regarding their conduct towards their masters. He finishes his discourse In I Peter 3, by saying the wives ought to submit to their husbands in the same way.

That word froward means willfully contrary. So even if your husband is obstinate or difficult, he deserves respect, because God said it. As believers, our life language is to give people more than they deserve. That's how God cares for us. And He asks us to love others the way He loves us. That's a pretty profound request. But God would not have asked it if it were not possible.

St. John 13:34 KJV reads A new commandment I give unto you, That ye love one another; <u>as I have loved you</u>, that ye also love one another. (Emphasis mine.)

Men are always attracted to honor. If you want your husband to treat you better, honor him. Don't wait to give honor until after you've been given something you desire. Honor him now. Today. Speak those qualities in existence that are absent in his life. On most occasions, He will rise to the place of honor. He will aspire to live up to the honor you give.

It is hard for a man to love a woman who disregards him. He may do it (as he should), but there is another level of connection that comes when she honors him. You make it easier for him to obey God when you reverence your husband.

Now I understand it's not always easy to honor those who mistreat us or fail to love us, but it is possible. And God expects us to do it. If we are asked to love our enemies, certainly, God expects us to love our disobedient husbands.

Our relationship with God cannot be based on our relationship with our husbands. "God, I will only obey you if my husband acts right." Our relationship with God must be independent. "Lord, I will serve you, no matter what my husband chooses."

Men who are raised to be unemotional - become unhealthy. They tend to come off as harsh, unloving, and indifferent. So how do you offer respect to a man who doesn't act like the husband you think you deserve?

You must first realize marriage is a ministry strictly limited to the earth. It is not a reward system for good and bad behavior. It has nothing to do with what is deserved. Besides, the Bible says none is good, but God. Relationships help us to serve Him better. What we receive from God, we give to our mates.

Secondly, you must forgive your husband. Let go of every offense he has *ever* brought to the marriage. Our Loving God forgives us and expects us to forgive all others - including our husbands. Ephesians 4:32 says, And be ye kind one to another, tenderhearted, forgiving one another, even as God for Christ's sake hath forgiven you.

Forgive him just like God forgives you, quickly and completely. In Matthew 6:15, it says that if we refuse to forgive, we won't be forgiven.

When I suggest this to wives, they usually counter, "But...what if he keeps offending me?" The answer is quite simple, you keep on forgiving him. We don't have a limited capacity to forgive. We have enough to last us for a lifetime. Our Gracious God continues to offer forgiveness to us.

A wife's lack of respect is no different than a husband's lack of love. The two actions are equally offensive to God and His Word. We often offer grace to ourselves and practice law with our husbands. We tend to judge their actions as unrighteous, while we give ourselves a 'mercy' pass.

Realize that you may have contributed to whatever problems exist in the relationship. Don't judge him. Love him by showing him the utmost respect. Not just once, but over and over again until it becomes a natural occurrence.

RESPECT HIM

In the case where a wife or her children are being abused, she should remove herself from that environment. It is not God's will for any person to be subject to abuse. The abuse is a sign that her husband is unhealthy. He needs help that the wife cannot give. She should seek safety for herself and her babies.

But for most situations - If we take our rightful place (submitted and respectful), more times than not, we can watch our marriages turn around.

4
WHAT ABOUT ME?

God has not forgotten you. Hebrews 6:10 (GW)

When I heard God ask me to honor my husband, I took offense. It was right smack dab in the middle of our recovery from the adultery that nearly destroyed our marriage. I thought God was unfair. I had been this 'faithful, godly' wife who had never entertained the idea of being with another man. Yet my husband had betrayed my heart. I wanted out. I didn't want to honor him. I wanted God to **handle** him. My flesh demanded justice. The pain of the adultery was just too intense and, in my estimation, did not warrant kindness. How could God ask me to honor someone like him? I thought it so unreasonable.

But I did love God and wanted to do what he asked. So I set out to do it out of mere obligation. I would prove that I, the self-sacrificing martyr, had done everything within my power to save my marriage. So if this marriage didn't last, it would be by my husband's hand. It is laughable now. But back then it wasn't so funny. I was indignant.

I placed myself on a holy pedestal and left my husband in sin's dungeon. He wasn't worthy of me, I thought. "I deserved better." Entitlement was looming.

It kind of felt like he was getting off easy after such a heinous sin against me. Treachery. Betrayal. It was the one thing that I said I wouldn't stick around for – adultery. And here I was stuck in it. Our marriage was damaged. Defective and broken. And I laid all of the blame at my husband's feet.

While adultery was not my sin of choice, I had other issues: Bitterness, pride, self-righteousness, a critical spirit, unforgiveness, etc. This was no short list.

I'm grateful that the Lord did not allow either of us to remain in the place we were. I grew in my understanding that I was no better than my husband. Jesus died for both of us. My sin was just as bad as his. I needed forgiveness as much as he did, if not more. He was at least contrite. I hadn't humbled myself, just yet.

When we began to deal with the cause of adultery, we found lust, insecurity, and pride at the base. It was a lethal concoction. My husband had to deal with those issues in his life. But when we got to the insecurity, I discovered that there were ways I had contributed. I didn't esteem him. I was critical and harsh. I was not a submitted wife.

While my husband was entirely responsible for his decision to go out on the marriage, I contributed to the unstable place that our marriage was in, in the first place.

Many in the church have distorted and misrepresented what God meant by submission. Submission was preached only to wives. There was nothing required of husbands. Submission was her duty, and she had no choice in the matter. It was demanded of her.

As a result, many wives despise submission and see it as a form of bondage. It's quite the opposite. Submission is not a curse, but an incredible blessing. It is an invitation to freedom. And God asks it of both men and women.

In the marriage relationship, the wife is to render submission to her husband. It is an act of love. God is not punishing wives, but looking out for us. Women are precious to the heart of God. He asks husbands to delight in us, tends to us, and love us in the same way he loves the church. For husbands to do that properly, he will need the cooperation of his wife. God never intended submission as a yoke but as a beautiful benefit. Wives submit in partnership with her husband. Together they are a team both submitted to God.

Submission is not for the leader's benefit to lord over his wife. Not in the least bit. Her Lord is her God. God asks wives to submit to make the huge responsibility of the husband bearable.

Submission has really gotten a bad rep. Because of that, wives can sometimes feel like they are getting the short end of the stick. What about my feelings? What about how he treats me? Where is my honor? It can feel oppressive and one-sided. Let me assure you, it is not. God does require that the husband honor the wife, as well.

Husband and wife are created equal. A wife is not a lesser human being. The scripture says we are joint-heirs. God, masterfully and delicately designed us.

However, the wife's function and responsibilities are not the same as her husband's. He is the head of the family, and that comes with loads of responsibility. He doesn't escape. God doesn't allow him to do whatever he chooses or mistreat his daughter. Absolutely not! God says he will not even hear his prayers if he doesn't handle his wife correctly. That's a tough reprimand for a leader. Heaven will close upon him and go silent.

Likewise, ye husbands, dwell with them according to knowledge, giving honour unto the wife, as unto the weaker vessel, and as being heirs together of the grace of life; **that your prayers be not hindered**. (I Peter 3:7 KJV) (Emphasis mine.)

Marriage is a two-way street. Yes, the wife renders submission, but there is also a heavy duty for the husband. He must take care of her, provide for her, honor her, and he must lead her in the same way that Christ leads the church - with love.

It is <u>never</u> the will of God for a wife to be abused, controlled, mistreated or manipulated.

WHAT ABOUT ME?

God has a perfect plan for your marriage, and it works well when both husband and wife submit to it. The ideal marriage has God front and center. Husband and wife come together as a team to love God and each other. Both husband and wife benefit when they follow the Lord's instruction.

Following God's word turned my whole life upside down. I watched my husband transform right before my eyes. He was so different. The more I respected him, the more he changed. It was pretty remarkable to experience. I followed the Word and called those things that be not as though they were. I prayed for him and rooted for him to win.

I didn't understand that what God was asking from me was for my advantage. I thought His request was aimed at my husband. When the Lord asked me to respect my husband, He was thinking of me and what He wanted for me. That's pretty awesome.

He wasn't discounting me or overlooking my needs. My needs were exactly what God had in mind. The respect I was to give my husband would affect him positively. This would cause me to reap the love that I so desperately needed. Not only would my husband be changed by respect, so would I. It has been mind-blowing.

I got the revelation. For my husband to lead me like Christ, he needed two things from me, submission and respect. As I rendered these two virtues to him, he would be transformed into an amazing husband.

Today, 38 years into our marriage, I tell everyone that my husband is the greatest man on the planet. And it is true. Our marriage has reached amazing pinnacles, and we are still growing and learning with each other. I feel thoroughly loved by this man. And I have even greater respect for him. He's not the same man I married, but he is a far better version of his former self.

We couldn't have gotten here if I had not been willing to die to my selfish flesh. I wanted my way. My flesh not only wanted revenge. I sought to get my husband told whenever I found it necessary. I wanted to correct his every error. So he didn't embarrass me or himself (mostly me). I wanted to reprimand him when he was toeing the line, and the list goes on. Thank God, I, too have been changed into another woman. As we both died, our marriage was able to come alive and flourish.

God always means us good, even when he asks us to do difficult things. My husband lavishly loves and dotes on me. He wants to make my every dream come true. I offer him respect without hesitation. I desire to be his dream wife. I want him to leave the earth thoroughly satisfied with the life we had together. I want him to feel like no other human being could have treated him better, respected him more, or blessed him more than I did. It is my aim to be the wife of his dreams.

5
WHAT IF HE'S WRONG?

The person who doesn't make mistakes is unlikely to make anything.—Paul Arden

Our husbands are anointed to lead us. It is his job to lead us closer to God. We have to believe and trust that. God called them to lead, then certainly He equipped them to do so. A man's job to lead is one that he has to *grow into*.

And the most challenging thing for a man is to lead his wife when she refuses to follow. It is difficult for him when he's attempting to follow God, and his wife is defiant. Most men will back down and surrender their leadership. As a wife, this is not what you want. You want your husband to follow God at all times, whether he hears God clearly or not. A godly husband is a benefit. Don't take that for granted.

God has a perfect plan for your life. It may be in the very thing you *want* to do that God says no…through your spouse. Or vice versa, the thing that we don't want to do that God says must be done.

We should not fight our husbands on it because we don't see it. Women do not lead the marriage. God will not show you everything. We must live by faith. That means respecting your husband's ability to hear the Lord speak. He may get it wrong, but God allows grace for that. You should, too.

As we yield to our spouses, we yield to our God. And God is at work producing something righteous within us both.

Husbands may feel like God is saying, go west. And you may want to go east. He could be 100% wrong in what he thought he heard. Don't make a big deal out of it, causing him to feel bad for missing it. That's not kind or righteous. But follow him as he attempts to follow God. Show him you support him and that you are on his side. It will build his confidence in his leadership. You have to give him room to make mistakes.

It creates a lot of undue pressure when a husband cannot err without his wife jumping all over his case. The wise wife says, "It's okay, honey. You will get it right the next time."

She doesn't say:

"I told you so."

"You should've listened to me."

"I was right."

"That's why I don't want to follow you."

Submitting to your husband does not mean that you have to agree with everything your husband says or does. It's appropriate for you to speak up when you disagree. Pray with him and for him. Share what you believe God is saying. However, say it with honor and leave it there.

Nagging him is never what is needed. You shouldn't try to force him to follow what you want or be bent on changing his perspective. Let God lead him.

Proverbs 27:15 A continual dropping in a very rainy day and a contentious woman are alike.

I have had conversations with many wives over the years. And it is unsettling to me when I encounter a wife who secretly hopes that their husband fails. Most often, it's when he doesn't do what she wants. This allows her to smugly say, "I told you so; you should've listened to me." Pride blinds her to her immaturity. It's not 'helper behavior' for a wife to want a cheap 'I-told-you-so' in exchange for a loss in her relationship. It could cost her more than she is willing to lose.

Respecting him means that you will always cheer for him to win, even if it means he goes against what you think. Ultimately when your husband wins, so do you.

Follow His lead and let the Holy Spirit be the Holy Spirit. The Holy Spirit knows how to convict and persuade him. And if your husband should miss God, which at some point, he will, the Lord is still at work, teaching him.

A prudent wife understands that if her husband is going in the wrong direction, she can go over his head by going down on her knees. She doesn't have to get mad at her husband or fuss at him. Better than all of that – she can pray for him.

I have witnessed the Lord changing my husband's mind when I have submitted to both – God and my husband. And at other times, it was my mind that was changed. So the best bet is to pray for your husband and rely on God to lead you both.

It is not wise to sulk or give off a lot of negative energy towards your husband because of a bad decision that he made. Even if what you advised was correct. He is still the leader. Be a team player. That means agree or not, I will go in the direction that he is leading – without kicking and screaming.

Your husband is the one you chose as the head of your home. So trust him. He's not perfect, but he needs you by his side. A man's most important need is for honor and respect. Make sure that you are genuinely lavishing it upon him, even when you disagree or don't understand.

When an immature wife doesn't like a decision, she sometimes focuses on some weakness or past failure of her husband. As if that will excuse her insolence. It won't. God still holds her accountable to submission.

His mistakes do not disqualify him from leadership. Often women are afraid that her husband's decision will cost the family. She resists his leadership because of this. But his mistakes are **growth opportunities**. No person comes into the marriage with full knowledge of how to handle every situation. However, if there is grace, he can learn and grow.

In the latter years of our married life, I would continually say to my husband, "If the ship goes down, I go down with it." I wasn't smart enough to say it earlier. But I did learn. Thank God. I have learned not to abandon the (relation)ship. That means I give my husband grace or room to make mistakes. I don't fuss because he gets it wrong. As, his dream wife, I understand that mistakes will be made. That's not an opportunity for me to pounce on them.

Our job is not to tell our husbands what he should do, how he should act, or what he should say. He is male. Therefore he is built differently than us. He will dissect and relate differently than a female. Let him be who God is making him to be.

When we took our vows, we said we were committed for *better and for worse*. It is not a multiple-choice phrase. 'For better and for worse' means 'come what may.' So when the worse part of your husband shows up (and it will), you need to commit to respecting him through it. And follow the path that God is leading through him.

Your husband will be more willing to take risks when he knows you are fully on his team. Risk-taking is a pre-requisite to success. You want your husband to take God-risks and not to stay safely tucked away on the sidelines. He has giants to slay and mountains to move. He needs a woman that will stand beside him and cheer him on.

However, there may be times that God will speak differently than what your husband is saying. At those times, God always trumps your husband. Ephesians 5:22 says wives submit to your own husbands, as to the Lord," **God is always due first obedience**. Certainly, the wife has no duty to submit to sin or to anything that goes against scripture. She must always choose what God says over what her husband says.

Nevertheless, that doesn't mean the wife gets to pick and choose when she will submit. She must obey her God. There may be times when God will speak to the wife to do something different than what the husband is saying. This is very sticky. And she must proceed with caution. Independent decision making should not be our default. God sees us as one. He expects wives to follow the leadership of their husbands. Yet there were times in scripture, where the wife had to or should have acted independently of her husband. These are unique examples:

Abigail had to go against the orders of her husband to follow God (I Samuel 25:14-34). God told Abraham to listen to Sara (Genesis 21:12) when she put Hagar and her son out. On the contrary, Sapphira submitted to her husband's request to lie to the Holy Spirit and had to share in the judgment of sudden death (Acts 5:1-11). Clearly, she should not have submitted to him.

So when those rare occurrences manifest, be sure to douse them in prayer. The main point is to follow God and not our own way.

6
THINK LIKE A WOMAN

Once I realized that right thinking is vital to victorious living, I got more serious about thinking about what I was thinking about and choosing my thoughts carefully. — Joyce Meyer

Have you ever heard the popular book title, Act Like a Lady Think Like a Man? It's intriguing, but it's not possible for a woman to do what the author is suggesting.

A woman is not wired to think like a man as much as she would like to. She is still female, and her brain works differently. So while it sounds good, it is just not possible.

Men usually tend to be singularly focused, thinking on one thing at a time, while a woman can think on many tasks at once. Men are logical thinkers, while women process more emotionally. Men are more analytical. They can think about a situation using only the facts. Women are a bit more challenged in this area. We may be distracted by our feelings and opinions on a particular subject. And the list of differences goes on. Neither is good or bad.

Ultimately men think like men and women think like women. So while we do not have the ability to think like a man, we can certainly seek to think better. Our goal should be to think like a woman…of God.

Thoughts direct us. So it is important to capture and guide our thoughts. The Bible tells us to cast down evil imaginations. What do you think about your husband? About your marriage? What are the thoughts that consume or torment you?

It is imperative that we think the right thoughts. Thinking negatively about our spouses will cause us to act negatively towards them. If you spend the day stewing in some offense that your husband caused, you will act on those ugly thoughts. As a woman of God, I have the power to arrest those thoughts. Because they aren't my thoughts, anyway. They come from the evil one who wants to destroy my relationship. I choose to meditate on good thoughts about my husband because our thoughts really do affect our feelings and behavior.

Think about what you want your marriage to look like and how you want to be the blessing that God intended. For that to happen, your mind must be renewed. You must be conformed into the image of God to think like a woman of God.

The Bible teaches us that out of the abundance of the heart, the mouth speaks (Luke 6:45). What you say comes from what you think. Our thoughts are responsible for the words we speak.

Psalm 19:14 is our prayer as wise wives, "Let the words of my mouth, and the meditation of my heart, be acceptable in thy sight, O LORD, my strength, and my redeemer."

Paul tells us in Philippians 4:8,9 to meditate on things that are true, honorable, right, pure, lovely, or admirable. And choose righteous behavior. This is how we maintain our peace.

If we understand that our thoughts generate our words, then we must grasp the idea that we must also watch our words. Words are powerful, and they can lift or lower. Words can change your life. A wife who continually complains, communicates failure to her husband. And most often, that is not her intention.

If you are tempted to say something derogatory to your husband, you can change a negative statement into a positive one. However, that requires that you stop to think before you speak. Don't just say what you feel. Consider the possible damage to your relationship.

Work to find a resolution. Most people can receive a positive suggestion quicker than negative criticism. You can bring up an issue without making it a complaint. For example, a complaint may be, "You never take me out on dates. Why can't we go out on dates like other married couples?" A better way to say it is, "Honey, I love spending time with you, can we have more time together?" As the old saying goes, you can draw more bees with honey. And you can bring a husband closer with sweeter words.

Mahatma Gandhi had something significant to say about thoughts that is still relevant for us today.

"Watch your thoughts, for they become your words.
Watch your words, for they become your actions
Watch your actions; they become your habits

Watch your habits for they become your character

Watch your character, for they become your destiny!"

It is our responsibility to intentionally think well of our husbands if we are going to love them properly. Let's not be hyper-focused on their issues or mistakes. It is better to mold our meditation. Point your thoughts toward the wonderful man he is.

If you want to do better, but find yourself saying things you told yourself that you wouldn't say, the problem lies within your thoughts. The Apostle Paul spoke of this problem in Romans 7:19, for the good that I would I do not: but the evil which I would not, that I do.

We've all found ourselves here at some point or another, wrestling with what is right. Paul continues in the following verses talking about the law that works against the law of his mind. We want to do right, but find ourselves doing wrong. So how do we break out of this unproductive cycle?

1. Start with repentance. Apologize to God first because he is the one who tells you to respect your husband. And so it is the Lord who you are offending first. Submit to Him. Ask for his help.

2. Repent to your husband. Tell him you are sorry, and you are working in this area of your relationship. That doesn't mean you will not make more of the same mistakes. Ask him to pray with you and for you. And to hold you accountable.

3. Seek out an accountability partner of the same sex. Choose someone wise and unbiased who can help you grow as a wife.

4. Choose to focus on the wonderful attributes of your spouse. Like his work ethic, his love for his children, his desire to please God, etc. Think good thoughts.

5. Be a gentle wife. Don't let words come flying out of your mouth, raw and uncut. Season your words. Let them be marinated with grace to make sure they are palatable. It is good always to take the time to hear your words before you speak them. Don't let them just fly out of your mouth because your emotions are out of control. We must practice patience and self-control.

Philippians 4:5 reads: Let your gentleness be apparent to all. The Lord is near. Our gentleness should be obvious. That takes practice.

To do this, you will have to go against what feels normal. Choose to do what is unnatural and uncomfortable to get a different result. If you have found yourself falling into old ill-mannered behaviors, you can change. As a believer, you can break generational curses and cultural influences.

Jesus became a curse for us so that we would have the victory over the enemy's power in our lives. If you start out disrespectful, you don't have to feel like there is no hope for you, because there is. The God of impossible things stands ready to heal and rectify. I didn't start as a respectful wife. It took me more than 10 years to get there. And I am still learning and growing.

Practice submitting to God, and you will find yourself much more submissive to your husband. And you will keep drawing your husband closer to yourself. Men go where they are celebrated and appreciated.

Ask yourself the following questions:

1. What thoughts am I thinking?

2. Are my words presented in a way that my spouse can hear me?

3. If he said the same thing to me, how would I feel/respond?

4. What does God think of the words I am using and my tone?

5. What does God think about my thoughts?

When we align ourselves with God's word, we can reap a holy union. We will see what God had in mind when He created marriage. You can be your husband's dream wife. It will take time. But if you commit to change, God will help you.

7
OUT OF CONTROL

Faith is having the courage to let God have control.
-Anonymous

This process of learning to respect our husbands and honor their leadership is immensely painful. I don't pretend that it is easy or smooth. It isn't. It will hurt your soul, and your flesh will scream in agony and opposition.

But it is exactly the place that God calls you to - sweet surrender. It's a regeneration of the soul. We all must be made over. And that means relinquishing control to Him. We don't lose control, but we must intentionally give it over to

Him. Our prayer should be, "Lord, I don't want to be in control." Then release it. We must be willing to let go of the reins and trust God in the process. We are safe in His hands. He created marriage and the rightful order of husbands and wives. Reaping the fruits of marriage depends on us depending on Him. We must lay our desires on the altar, knowing it is for our benefit. Our hope is to be conformed as we cling to Christ. We pray right along with the Psalmist, "Create in me a clean heart and renew a right spirit within me," Psalm 51:10.

This prayer is costly, but necessary. It will cost us our comfort and familiarity. God wants us to exchange them for something much greater.

Only when we die, can our marriages genuinely live and flourish. Death is an important element in marriage. The Apostle Paul said it best, "I must die daily." The flesh is disastrous to all relationships, but especially marriages. Death to 'me' as a spouse means life to 'us' as a married couple. But life to 'me' means death to 'us' or to our marriage. Oneness is produced in death.

Oneness is different than singleness. Oneness is about meshing two wills into one. Singleness is about individualism and being separate. Singleness in marriage yields selfishness. And selfishness produces death (divorce).

St. Matthew 10:39 He that findeth his life shall lose it: and he that loseth his life for my sake shall find it.

That doesn't mean you have to lose who you are, as a person, in the marriage. It's quite the opposite. God created you before you were ever married. So certainly you have your own identity. You don't lose that when you say, "I do."

However, when we come into marriage, we must kill that part of ourselves that is toxic and selfish - the sinful nature. Because we were born in sin and shaped in iniquity, we all have that ugly part.

We have to decide, do we empower the uncomely part and hold on to the leadership of our lives? Or do we let go and trust God? It's ultimately our choice.

It's scary to abandon control, but it is certainly worth it. You really can trust God. He has a better plan and a better method. We can experience marriage at its best if we choose to execute it God's way.

Marriage on my terms did not work out. My husband and I were up and down, arguing most of the time. Our home lacked peace.

I was tearing my husband down with my thoughts and words. He was passive-aggressive and detached from me. The battle for control was epic. We were just one big mess. Our marriage was not at all what God had in mind.

Things came to a head in our relationship when adultery was uncovered. We had to stop and decide to readjust some things if we were going to move forward. It forced us to change how we were relating. It wasn't quick, and it wasn't easy.

We wanted God's plan, but we weren't living by it – not fully. We were very mediocre in our relating to God. Our prayer life was hit or miss. We read the Word but didn't give much time to studying it.

There was no evidence of the fruit of the Spirit in our lives. We did whatever we felt when we felt it. Both of our flesh was governing the relationship. And the Lord received no glory.

God asked me to give up control. He wanted me to be "out of control." That meant stepping aside and trusting Him with every part of my life. My 'yes' meant I agreed to let the Lord make my husband into His image. What my husband looked like was not up to me. How he conducted himself was not my responsibility. I had to leave it all up to God. That was difficult for an insecure woman. Insecure people seek to be in control because it gives them certainty.

The Lord began me on the journey to surrender. It started with practical things. He told me to get rid of the secret stash of money I kept hidden – for emergencies. He said it was a sign that I didn't trust Him or my husband. I inhaled deeply and obeyed. I was afraid, but I wanted God's way.

I had to trust God first in order to trust my husband. And it wouldn't happen overnight. My husband was very lackadaisical with our finances. But God required a change from me. He didn't want me to wait until my husband changed. The Lord had come for my transformation right at that moment. In essence, He was saying, "Give everything to me even when you don't know how it's going to work out." I said, "Yes."

I stopped selling my husband out to bill collectors. The in-control version of myself would tell them how irresponsible my husband was. I would side with the creditor and then pay the bill. "He's so irresponsible. I don't know why he didn't pay that bill." My words didn't sound like one who was in love and in covenant. But my out-of-control makeover caused my words to change. I started saying, "My husband must have overlooked that bill, call him, he is honorable. He will take care of that." And he did. My husband stepped up to the plate.

Previously in our marriage, he paid bills when he felt like it, not when they were due. My credit score (which was high) went plummeting down right beside his. It was part of what was required in letting go.

I needed some humility. I wore my credit score like it was some type of badge of honor. God had to prove to me what was more important. My husband has more value than that score. It was an incredible lesson. Today, we both have excellent credit.

My makeover included me having to stop telling my husband how to drive, where to turn, what to say on the phone, when to pray, how to be a better dad or a better husband, and how his serving God should look. I relinquished it all. It was never my job, but a result of my insecurity. That's a God-sized job, too big and too heavy for a wife.

We somehow get it in our heads that we are the ones to change him or prod him to maturity. After all, God did say we were to be the "helper." We have certainly misunderstood that role. Fortunately, helping our husbands is so much easier than that. We must leave the tough stuff to the Lord. We get to love, admire, support, cheer, and respect him. The journey to stepping out of control is uncomfortable and sometimes painful, but immensely necessary. Being out of control causes order to come into our lives in a way we have never experienced. And that's where God wants all of His daughters – out of control. Leave the Chief seat for Him. He does know what He is doing.

8
BODY MINISTRY

Just by your touch, you make me forget the rest of the world. – Anonymous

Sex is good. God created it and gifted it to a husband and wife on their wedding day. It is the emotional connection that helps couples bond physically. A healthy sex life can boost the marriage, but it must be based on mutual love and respect.

Many times we can send wrong sexual messages and communicate disrespect in a way we don't intend. We must communicate often about expectations in the bedroom.

When we talk things out, it conveys trust and understanding. So that we don't guess or think something that is untrue. It's the way to keep the enemy out.

Some things that wives need to understand about your husband's sexuality:

<u>Sex helps him feel good about himself.</u> It is tied to his image as a man and a higher priority on his list. Sex helps him think clearer and helps his creative juices to flow. So be available to him and don't talk down to him about his performance. Avoid criticizing him, especially in the moment. If there is something you need to talk about, take time to frame your words so that they aren't hurtful and pray about the best time to bring it up.

<u>He feels loved when his wife is open to him sexually.</u> Sex ties him to his wife. When a wife gives her husband sexual attention, it helps him to be more attentive to her. It is a way of connecting to her emotionally. And it boosts his mood.

<u>Husbands don't want to feel like they are a bother to their wives when requesting sex.</u> If a wife is irritated by his request, she is sending a message to him that may not be intended. She may be physically tired, emotionally overwhelmed, or experiencing pain. Instead of shooing him away, take time to explain in detail what your real issues are. When not given an explanation, sometimes husbands will internalize the rejection. When you cannot be intimate with your husband, let him know when you expect to be available (i.e., within the next 48 hours).

<u>Husbands tend to desire sex more frequently than their wives.</u> Seasons in marriage change, resulting in a change in sexual appetites. Be sensitive to that. But in general, husbands tend to want sex more often. It is best to accommodate him as much as possible. The frequency of your connection will change with the seasons of your marriage. But make loving his body a priority. Remember, it is a compliment, not an insult that your husband wants to express his love to you.

RESPECT HIM

Husbands don't want to be punished or manipulated by their wives. It is crucial not to allow disagreements to stop you from connecting to him, sexually. You should avoid withholding sex to get your way. Sex was never designed to be used as a weapon or manipulation against him. Sex is for loving him, not chastising, or teaching him. The scriptures even admonish us not to abstain from one another without consent. (I Corinthians 7:5)

Your husband cannot possibly satisfy you sexually without your cooperation. You must be involved in the process. What you think about him will determine how you respond to him. As a man (or woman) thinketh in his (her) heart, so is he (she). (Emphasis mine.) Our meditations determine our actions. A wife must intentionally think good thoughts about her husband, and she must prepare herself to receive him.

Think about his whole body and what you enjoy about it. Desire takes practice for women, not for men. If you are directing your thoughts about your husband, you can stir up desire towards him. A husband is blessed when he walks into his bedroom, and his wife is supercharged with desire for him. Put forth the extra effort to love your husband.

<u>Men are visual and want to look at their wives' bodies.</u> So be careful about jumping in your comfy flannel pajamas every night. Be his eye candy. Let him see you in lingerie that is just for him. He will appreciate it. Sometimes cut on the lights. Let him see you. All of the things we, as women, obsess over, men don't even notice. So don't point it out. Cellulite, varicose veins, stretch marks, and excess body weight do not deter your husband. He still wants your body.

<u>Men liked to be touched.</u> Studies show that all humans need touch to thrive emotionally. It is said we need 8 touches per day. So purposely touch him. Rub his head. Hug him. Kiss his lips. Caress his face. Massage his shoulders. Minister to his full body. Let him know that you are all in. Touch him often. Communicate your love in more than words.

RESPECT HIM

Never make him feel that he repulses you. Let no part of your body reject his. Let your hands represent love to him and let your touch always bring comfort.

9
HIS DREAM WIFE

Loving you is a privilege, Knowing you is a blessing, being with you is a dream come true.- Anonymous

Before an artist puts her paintbrush to the canvas, she has the picture already in her mind. The architect draws the plans before the builder builds. In that same way, as wives, we have to imagine what type of wife we want to be. A nagging, overbearing, screaming wife or a wise, respectful, supportive wife? If you paint that picture in your mind of what you want to be for him, then you can live it out in front of him. He will even see you the way you see yourself – the girl of his dreams.

It certainly will take some work. If you are willing to put the work in, you can reap the benefits. If you truly want to become his dream wife, you will have to see yourself that way, first.

What does a dream wife look like?

She…

D efers to him. She seeks his wisdom and follows his leadership. According to Ephesians 5:23, Christ is head of the church, and the husband is head of the wife.

She does not buck against the word, but fully embraces her husband as the head of their family.

Wives, submit yourselves unto your own husbands, as unto the Lord. For the husband is the head of the wife, even as Christ is the head of the church: and he is the saviour of the body. Therefore, as the church is subject unto Christ, **so let**

the wives be to their own husbands in everything. (Ephesians 5:22-25 KJV) Emphasis mine.

She hears her husband's heart and not just his words to assess what his true desire is. Then she follows it. Sometimes men will say something they don't mean. Every husband should say what he means, but while he's still growing, his dream wife will not have a problem with trying to discern his true heart.

R espects him at all times, even when she feels he isn't acting as he should. If she has an issue, she takes it to the Lord first, to find the right words and the right time to bring it up. She approaches her husband without accusing or attacking him. She is gentle to bring up an issue in a way that he can receive it. Her objective is to find a resolution.

Proverbs 25:11 A word fitly spoken is like apples of gold in pictures of silver.

She doesn't override his authority if he commits to complete some task but leaves it undone. As much as she may want to have someone else do it, she waits on him. Because she understands that will do more harm to her marriage.

She doesn't undermine her husband's authority with the children or anyone. Once he sets a directive, as his teammate, she works with him to make sure it is followed through.

When she disagrees, she does not manipulate him or throw a temper tantrum to get her way. She knows how to respectfully disagree as a mature woman of God.

The dream wife does not use anger to pressure her husband to change his mind. She trusts God to get him where he should be.

E ncourages him in his dreams and aspirations. She prays with him about the things he wants to achieve. She is supportive even if she can't see it at the moment. She works with him on his plan to make his dreams a reality.

A pplauds him. And she appreciates his efforts to make her happy. She praises her husband regularly. Most men will repeat behavior that is praised. Marriages thrive in an atmosphere of praise. It's a critical discipline to create within your home. And no one understands this better than the dream wife.

She chooses to be his number one cheerleader, above all others. She is the one who is most likely to applaud him. No one praises her man more or louder than she.

She says thank you, and please, always exemplifying good manners to him. She doesn't take any of his kindness for granted.

M akes a home for him. She makes her home a place of respite, where her husband looks forward to retreating. She keeps order and directs the children to pick up after themselves. Not only is it clean, but there is tranquility in her home. She creates an atmosphere of peace to encourage him to be anxious to come home every day.

She allows a time for him to unwind before she brings up issues.

She stays within the family budget and helps to cut expenses so that he doesn't have unnecessary stress.

W ows him! She is affectionate and makes herself physically attractive and available to him. She takes care of herself. She puts in the effort to look good and smell good for him. She understands her husband wants to be desired by her. So she doesn't just wait for his initiation. She approaches him for physical intimacy.

I ntercedes for him. She stands in the gap for her family. She covers her husband in prayer, and she doesn't complain to others about his flaws. But she goes to the One who can make a difference.

She prays every day for him and the concerns that weigh him down. She prays for him to grow in his leadership of the family.

She lives by Philippians 4:6-7 Be anxious for nothing, but in everything, by prayer and petition, with thanksgiving, present your requests to God. And the peace of God, which surpasses all understanding, will guard your hearts and your minds in Christ Jesus.

The dream wife depends on God. If there is something, she needs or desires, she doesn't worry about it or pressure your husband for it. She is a praying woman, so she asks her Heavenly Father for it. God is her source. She understands that she can ask her husband for something, but she looks to God to provide it. She is not uptight about some need unfulfilled. She let's all of her requests be made known unto God.

RESPECT HIM

F aithful. She's trustworthy and loyal. She does not look to another man for attention or help. If she needs attention, she asks her husband for it. She doesn't flirt or threaten him that she will get it from someone else.

The wise wife also keeps her husband's confidence and shows that she can be trusted with his secrets. She shares them with no one. And she doesn't use them against him in a dispute. If he knows he can trust her, he will continue to share with her. If she betrays him, she can be assured; he won't share again.

E njoys her marriage. She compliments him regularly. She plans activities for the two of them. She surprises him with little things and plans dates for the two of them. She celebrates him, and she looks for wonderful ways to praise the amazing man he is.

~~

Becoming his dream wife all starts with being God's vision of a daughter. The closer we follow God, the better we will be in all of our relationships. I am not suggesting that you have to be perfect. But rather that you love him perfectly (the way God loves you). Give him the best of you.

Marriage is ministry. And we serve God by serving our men. The harmonious marriage is where the husband and wife are challenged to out-serve each other, putting the other above themselves. Have fun, enjoy one another, and God will be glorified.

10
THE BEST PART

A wife's prayers for her husband have a far greater effect on him than anyone else, including his mother's. (Sorry, Mom) —Stormie Omartian, The Power of a Praying Wife

Too often wives want to change their husbands. Sure there are areas we hope they will grow in. However the wise wife knows that real change comes through prayer. And no one should pray more or stronger for our husbands than we.

Put in the time to pray for your husband. It's your most important work as a wife. We should pray daily for them.

While this sounds obvious, it is an area that is most neglected by married couples. We need and depend on the Lord to help us bring forth the change in our own lives. So how do we think it will happen for our mates? If you are new to prayer, you can start with 5 minutes a day. You will find there are so many prayer points, it is most likely that you won't stay at 5 minutes.

Pray for his walk with God, his leadership as a husband, and his parenting skills. Ask God to give him wisdom and to keep his character. Pray for his weaknesses and healing and wholeness as a man. Pray against attacks of the enemy. Pray for success on his job and in his ministry. Include his relationships with family and friends. The list is almost limitless. Be intentional and create the time to stand in the gap for your husband.

It's also important to pray for yourself. God has a picture in mind of the wife that He wants you to be. There are areas that we will all need to grow in. Being a wife is no small challenge. You want to be an asset to benefit your husband and not interfere in the work that God is doing in him. That means, we too, will need wisdom and direction. We will need to be patient and exercise restraint. We need to pray for our own weaknesses and the areas we need healing in. It is our aim to die to our own desires and let God be glorified in us and in our relationships. Prayer is the best work we can do for our marriages.

The following is a catalyst to help you get started.

A Wife's Prayer

O Lord, I lift up to you my love, my friend, and leader. Forgive me, Lord, for speaking harshly to him. Forgive me for not allowing him to be the man you've called him to be. Forgive me for interfering with his walk and his ministry. Deliver me O Lord from unforgiveness and rashness of words. Help me to be submissive to him, to be quick to hear and slow to speak. Cleanse me from my flesh, O Lord that wants to hold grudges and recall the past.

RESPECT HIM

Lord fill my mouth with pleasant words that will encourage him and lift him up. Let my tongue be filled with the law of kindness. And let me do him good and not evil all the days of my life.

Lord, this is my husband. Let there be no time in his life that I tear him down. Help me, O Lord, to build him up and to walk in holy submission unto him. Teach me how to trust him, how to make him shine, and to love him.

Lord, this is my husband that you've created for me. May I never disrespect him, but honor him. May I never damage his spirit, but encourage him. May I never expect him to meet all of my needs; but may they be met in you. Let my love give him confidence so that he does safely trust in me. When our journey together is complete, Dear Lord, may he arise up, call me blessed and praise me in the gates.

In Jesus' name, I pray. Amen

ABOUT THE AUTHOR

Crystal Jones has been wildly in love with her husband, Oscar Jones, for more than 38 years. The dynamic duo has led Marriage for Lifetime Ministries for 28 years, ministering to marriages across the country and abroad. Crystal and her husband are the parents of 7 (including 1 daughter-in-law and 1 son-in-law) and grandparents of 9. The two have authored many books together and apart. They have spoken nationally and internationally. Oscar and Crystal have been on radio and television, rallying for marriages to thrive for a lifetime.

www.ingramcontent.com/pod-product-compliance
Lightning Source LLC
Chambersburg PA
CBHW051658040426
42446CB00009B/1192